i.m. my father,

Frederick Harvey Johnston

Acknowledgements

Acknowledgements are made to the following publications, where some of these poems first appeared:

The Irish Times; Irish Studies Review (Bath); *Irish University Review; The Big Spoon; The Honest Ulsterman; Cencrastus* (Scotland); *Chapman* (Scotland); *Poetry Ireland Review; WP Monthly* arts review; *The Clifden Anthology; The Independent* (London); *Orbis; New Letters* (USA); *The Southern Review* (USA); *Cyphers; The Seneca Review* (USA); *Verse* (USA); *Galway Advertiser; Books Ireland; Writing in the West* (Connacht Tribune); *The New Welsh Review; Poetry Now; Asylum.*

In a photograph he squints ahead
To a future from which we've gone.

Sean Dunne, *Sydney Place* ('Railings')

... the sure acre where my sense is true,
while round its boundaries sprawl the screes of doubt.

John Hewitt, *Substance and Shadow*

Contents

Driving in Silence

All around us, like a black dream with no waking
    Connemara under dark rain, headlights making
    mute pleas for leniency, drenched trees shaking

Nothing to hear, as if all sound had been exiled
    air rushing through a tired engine; you smiled
    as the car heated up, then slept snug as a child

Road dipping, folding, turning, rat's squeak of wipers
    home between the new-built bungalows; others
    like ourselves evaporate past in a hiss of wet tyres

A coastal country, a void among rocks, a poet's wail
    a lament for emigration, a need, a love gone stale –
    all this we hurry from into the merchants' city, our Pale.

Shop Street, Winter Morning

This is the first shutter to go up
like an eyelid, the street not yet awake
the scarred wood of the scrubbed chopping-block
rises and falls like hayfields seen from the air

This early, there is no scent of blood
that comes later when the fridge door opens
now the shop-front's shining like a theatre
in a field hospital an hour before the Big Push

Newspapers in tight bundles wrapped in string
sit mute in doorways waiting for the knife
office-girls made more desirable by sleep
scatter in flat shoes past a Chinese take-away

Now the gleaming hooks are on the rail
for an instant they rock and tinkle like small bells
new sawdust is thrown in handfuls on the floor
the morning smells of dead meat before the sun rises.

To A Daughter In Her Seventeenth Year

'We are still living in pawn.'
 – Ulick O'Connor, *Easter Week 1986*

I am of Ireland: there is weight to that
Something you can balance with, but what
Does it mean?

> Harps and shamrocks only,
> Something vaguely green?

A world in easy reach, we redefine
Ourselves in terms of where we've gone
And what we've seen –

> I sent you books on being
> Irish, a sense of history

In an effort to reclaim for you
A sort of past, a place to remember
Without maps

> Behind the brash visa stamp
> A quiet poetry

But something to build on, a clue
To what you are when you need to know
A safe place to go

> To rummage in and gather up
> Your own story –

It will be different from mine and from
The packaged history of your birth country
Different and more glad

    Rooted still in half-remembrance
    The half-light of mythology.

Baling Out
for Jacques Rancourt

We drove over airfields the Americans had built
In a war he remembered like a chapter from a book
    he turned and reversed in miles of concrete space
    as if taking a new freedom by the scruff of the neck
    the rusted hangar doors tongued in outrage
    at each squall and feathering of weather coming on
    calling up their missioned adolescent dead

Silence and a Sunday heat filled our family car
Like water, as if we'd skidded off a bridge to drown
    the windows refused to open for a dozen miles
    and I grew nauseous and fought it in my shame
    only to throw up in the kitchen sink
    and lie then on the bed in watery evening light
    watching my Airfix fighters dogfight on a thread

He said one day he'd watched the real thing happen
He'd stood in a street and stared up at the smoke
    twenty years had passed but it was clear
    a Spitfire rasping through a Belfast sky
    doodling back and forth across paper clouds
    and he'd wondered what had happened
    to the pilot, if he'd died, or baled out instead –

I lined up half-naked with the others in a tin hut
We coughed when told to and did an eye-test
    frisky rain belted the wired glass windows
    what I remember most is the cold embarrassment
    my eyes had floaters and that let me out
    I'd never fly, but there was always ground crew
    I could think about it, call back: I never did.

Curse

His pacing from the bed to the window
You're right, you're right, I know all that

an out-of-focus gazing at the rampant grass
a smell like ether poised at the edge of things

he longed for a cigarette, it was forbidden
a half-drunk bottle of Lucozade, something

lying in ambush behind the plastic curtains
This gut ache, he said, *that will not go away*

later, a hell-scene in a private room,
strapped into a cot with metal sides,

hair gone, the steady beat of a suction pump
eyes blindly mad overnight, arms

mummied-up in bandages, he was eating
away the pain, going out too slowly, roomful

of pretty nurses, the kind he'd crack jokes
at, iron in the clammy hot air, shrinking visibly –

for a week hard men in pubs drank to his memory
who'd stepped over him often in the street

he was a wild man, he was some tulip,
a quare tongue on him, isn't the drink a curse?

Clio

She was the quiet one
played the violin
entered a room with poise and grace
the old women whispered of sin

They shook the lavender
from their bony laps
she sat in a chair by the French windows
being very English, called us *chaps*

Her death, like her marriage
appeared in *The Times*
(it was on Special Offer in Ireland then)
some polite condolences, two curious rhymes

Her coffin, I remarked
had been peculiarly small
as if no full-grown woman lay within
but a child-sized Victorian doll

Death by drowning
they say, brings songs
all sorts of music, rhapsodies and fugues
I can't imagine it lasts all that long

And the sea off the pier
was November rough –
you all know what that sort of sea's like
one good mouthful's enough

But Clio was musical
(very precise on scales)
she'd have known if the music was heavenly
or merely the humping of whales.

Don Cristobal's Dream

'. . . .an army that keeps searching
for the name of God?'
 – Carlos Suárez, *Icarus*

Don Cristobal rode back from a routine tour
Of his vast cattled acres and, dismounting, said:
'I am, of course, all your fathers and all the dead.'

And said nothing more until, unattended, hard-
Breathing, he pushed his way like a fat Spring tide
Through their gapes and stares and the front door

And collapsed into one of his ancestors' Toledo chairs –
'I will decide (he shouted) what to do with the world!
I have seen God's face and he looks just like me! I'll

Kill with my bare hands any who'll dare disagree –
I'll smother their children at birth – I am hard as a
Bull, I am Don Juan, I am glorious as adultery!'

A vulture sat on his shoulder. The sun went down.
A servant shook Don Cristobal, he woke: 'Throw
Me a rope, or I'll drown!' He sat up, looked around.

'I was dreaming,' he said, 'You do believe me?'
Wordless, the servant withdrew, the vulture flew away –
'I am dying,' said Don Cristobal: 'And you all leave me.'

Shed

for my father

His toolshed without his eagerness to work in it
gave up its bladed shine and hammer sureness

planking splintered, nails festered, both
with time became less useful and more dangerous.

The Old Colonials

We'd dared its broken walls before
But this was different, as if lifted on flights of air
We took possession, thinking of girls but obstinate
In the face of being real men
      we broke empty picture-frames
      under our guttees
      not knowing the old colonials had
      named even what we used to walk on

All that clotted red brick, a peeling door
A wardrobe beckoning with a blind mirror stare
Plaster dust rising and falling in white sunlight
A rusting biscuit-tin, a fountain pen –
      things that had relinquished names
      abandoned identities
      a green-leather writing pad
      but no desk under it to lean on

Then we found the photos on a bit of tiled floor
Someone kicked something and there they were
Sepia-tones, faded ornate edging gold-leafed in spite
Of time, weather, plundering schoolboy-men –
      a family playing racket games
      long skirts, wide hats, exotic trees
      the most beautiful girls we had
      ever seen smiling at us brazenly

We went home about then, dropped the photos more
Or less where they'd first taken shape, or appeared
It was hard to say: the dark came down, it was night
Too quickly, we never visited the house again
                    and found no names
                    for the ghosts we had to appease
                    who lived in us now, calm and sad
                    unpacking themselves in time for tea.

Before Truth

'Speaking is easy. . . '
  – Philippe Jaccottet, *Speech*

Before truth, there was magic
        and that is how they lived

The shy girl, the older man
        reaching but never touching

Under a mad moon he opened
        his mouth and his heart flew out

Like a caged bird stunned by
        freedom, it circled and fell

She saw the shattered workings,
        secret nuts and bolts of his being

And learned to look him in the eye,
        shy no longer, no longer girlish

No magic now, a cold sharp logic
        cuts them apart: time passes.

Repudiation

To have these walls to live within
And cultivate their silence and restraint
Repudiate the letter and the book review
Misdirected anger and unfair complaint –

Make tea at four and read until Angelus
With one hand warmed by sunlight on a chair
Make a quick trip out for the evening paper
Spread it on the carpet and leave it there

To make no sound detectable without
Never seen at a window or heard to sing
Barely to hear the rumours going round
About some local crime or other sordid thing

To render oneself harmless and invisible
By act of will and discipline
So that when the knock comes and the question
One can say in truthfulness there's no one in.

Old Boaz

Old Boaz grumbled in his cups
of worlds others conquered because of his maps

And when he stumbled out the door
he left a trail of beery slobber on the tavern floor

The earth was flat, round it ran the sun
there were heresies, holy burnings, all kinds of fun

When Boaz died he lay three days unfound
the sweet tang of death brought the watch around

They broke the planky door
and he was spread across his maps upon the floor

They hadn't been aware
that maps can kill. Such occurrences were rare

A priest was called, who swore
the maps were drawn up in their victim's gore

The place was burned at once
old Boaz too. The devil's work leaves no room for chance.

Consider Boaz and his maps
he dumped the round world's knowledge in their laps

got drunk and died
and who can say his profane cartography lied?

those who used him fared quite well
they gave us Hiroshima, Hot Dogs and Rock 'n' Roll.

Poetry

After rain, a reluctant moon
night-flowers open, wet grass –

does one, in middle-age, put
on poetry like surgical stockings?

I'm in a snug door-bolted place
wondering about this and that

when you ask me about
the act of writing, is this what you mean?

At a window men's voices
argue their way home – small hours,

small enough to roll in your fingers
and swallow like couscous

O small-faced Irish man!
To dream of the world while dangling

from Europe's lip is no small conceit.
Back to your books, your girl,

let your poets voyage for you
they'll invent the world as they go along.

The North Remembered

Sundays were different, a week's slowing.
I'd walk to visit cousins, shortbread fingers
On the rim of a saucer, tea spilling over with dignity

White-gloved, they sat on the edges of chairs
Waiting for something, a signal, a door opening
And the parlour moved around them into afternoon

Envious, unsure, I picked up what was left
Of all that promised future and abandoned them,
Dragging a lumped sack of smugness after me

Into exile. One gets older, needs more, sees
The significance in what that ordered primness owned:
To be two-hearted is no simple island matter –

When we sit and break out those syllables again
Those arched wee churchy consonants and line's end rise
I circle back to what makes up my other half

Splice the severed ends of distancing and time
Connect and in some small way balance out
What's been fragmented, cowped off centre, set on edge.

Straddling

To know a settling place
    a gate that rests your elbows
    and a view that dominates your next move
    a gesture over a wall that punctuates
    the given word, the agreed signature –
to have all this from birth is a sort of peace

As not having it cuts to the bone
    roots to the quick the hesitancy
    in the heart, as if no steering were ever
    possible over the scraggled charts
    you stuffed in pockets of memory, hazarding
a guess each time, always edging, bordering

What I know is this –
    our reach is never what we think it is
    and no wall we build is utterly unbreachable:
    sometimes a doubt is all that saves us
    sends us running to where the fault lies –
straddling beyond our span we fall over always.

Crossing the Bann

Narrow enough here to leap across
Or so you'd think, a small green illusion
The trees make dipping in and out of shadow
We crossed that abrupt wee bridge back
And over a dozen times that day –

I have a held broken remembrance
Of three women rehearsing wedding hymns
At an upright piano, and I took myself off
To read in a lapsed armchair under
The slow meticulous click of a cranky antique clock.

In the village church a plaque recalled
A half-dozen men lost in a world war, and
One stained window over from it another named
A victim of a recent local ambush, black
Mottled stone and gold lettering

I had begun to read when the first notes
Of something by Handel lumbered over the
Polished prayer-booked pews. I knew the shared
Sense of siege which hedged us in, felt the cold
Stagger of geography shoulder me off centre –

Driving in the night, again the river
A bridged obstacle, a sliver of blue on a map
The doors-locked wee halls crouching in fields
The warnings to repent nailed to roadside trees
The familiar foreignness of it all is what

Struck home. Hard enough not to stop,
Get out, look over the fence just for the feel
Of it, your tongue already wrapping
And unwrapping the syllables coming back to you –
All that wanting and not wanting can toss a man.

You chisel the question and it stays –
What if the choice were really yours, and
All the coming and going found its resolution
In some place like this, a bridge under you
To keep you neither here nor there?

Adopted Things
for Sylvia

You go North now in your wintering flight
By wintering fields
To familiar townlands
And the welcome of known windowlight

In our small exile we turn round
To the recognisable
The tongue remembering makes speech
In its first vernacular, its birthing ground

I remain in the clutter of adopted things
An attic in the heart
Where indecipherable maps dust away
Dry mothworked air, small hoverings

Like a need for the fullness of bread
A hunger comes
Not bellyheavy
But greedier, a hunger in the head

I would lift my cousin's gloved hand
And hold it to the light
Scrutinise the frail bonewhite lacing
Prayer book in her bag, her Sunday planned

I am rooted in what's disinherited
Something earthed
In the unattainable: I sing still
In the Sunday school I never visited

A word seeds this odd history
A chance phrase side-mouthed
Spades the indistinct familiar
Turns the moist soil of memory.

Caoin

Where in this dark can light be found
When she of earth, rock, river and blown bush
Has gone underground –
          Of her singing voice, no sound?

No light or brightness on the road of the world
No woman like her by window, hearth, door or bed
The wheat-haired girl
          Her hair new-washed, new-curled

And I imagine light to loosen dark thinking
So that I might stand up straight again and live
Of love's cup drinking
          My heart to float, my soul sinking.

Tie Up Your Hair

Tie up your hair, loved girl, come with me
I have a memory as bright and leaping
                as the sun on a salmon's back
                I have watched you sleeping

Let down your hair, girl, for the world to see
I have a memory of your hair sweeping
                the pillow like sun on corn
                and I wide-eyed, weeping.

Wood

O young love, be good
    be full of longing as a windy wood

Be full of anger as
    one poet envying what another has

Be at your best when
    your poet sickens and neglects his pen

And if your love dies
    go quietly, leave him where he lies

But for now, love, be good
    full of whispers as a windy wood.

Breaking

Your hair over a pillow, slivers
    of winter sun on a frosted window

That first breaking of the heart, when
    love beak-taps and pecks, and departs

Do not put your arms around me, I said
    no more of that, if you can't love me.

My Love Asleep

All the daft day's riot falters here
The lake of her silence is deep,
         motionless and clear

Unlike my own small well of wide-eyed spite
Perturbed, unfathomable, black
         as a winter's night.

Dragon's Teeth

'In all her finery, the king's daughter. . . .'
  – John Heath-Stubbs, *Four Dragons*

You say the notes of night are musical
I say not –
They are the hissing of steam from a cracked
pot, somewhat redeemed
by your voice in the half-light street

A child's alchemy motivates the stars
and old God
is the worming stone blind life of the new-turned
sod, pod-bellied wife
to adulterous rain and drunken storm

Rain's runny clattering down the drain
a new moon
served up to the dribbling sky like ice cream on a
spoon, a lunatic cry
sounds from door to door and is dissolved

You visit me, love, with your gift of smoke
but I know
the ghost that hides there in the heart's after-
glow, his slow grin
opens like a window, a dragon-toothed invitation.

From the Irish, Perhaps

No peace now that love has gone
No place of comfort, no going home

Singing I miss, and your own tune
Your laughing voice in a loud room

Your bright eye across a full table
Your fingers on my arm in passing

My empty bed is lit by a red moon
No sleep for me on the softest down

Day I dread for its useless duties
Night for its wide hours of self-pity

You were my hour of sun in winter
The full wineglass, the brimming pitcher

Your going put the dark in me
Killed the light I'd guarded jealously

Nothing is new now, everything is old
The summer is windy and wet and cold.

Middle

'That he should opulently inherit
The goods and titles of the extinct.'
  – Robert Graves, *A Country Mansion*

He forgets where he put the car. Then finds it
Parked between two straight white lines –
How ordered the world is, when it tries!

Six o'clock – a radio Angelus reminds him
Of a neat-rounded day closing off, vague
Things done in a paperclip-and-memo sort of way

The longest summer he can remember, girls
Dressed to kill, a pseudo-tropical atmosphere
Of events occurring under a dark glamour

A cardboard tree swings like a censer from
The dashboard, the car's hot interior smells like
A lavatory bowl rinsed with disinfectant –

I didn't bargain for this, he says out loud:
Reading bright novels on sunny afternoons
Driving for ever to nowhere through the same crowd

The knowledge of what the middle actually is:
A standstill point between the other man's field
And the unseedable arid acre you're starving in

He stalls at traffic-lights in third gear
Behind him a disapproving, better centred world
Gets ready to horn this Quasimodo off the road

And someone tell me where it ends:
Can I pick up where I left off back then
When there was hope of some kind, and it rained?

The Family House

The family house is no longer there
Some say it never was
Walls, light-switches, framed photos
Tables and chairs
The mythical built-in comfort clause

A sullen child in a corner armchair
I heard its Saturday roar
Closed ears to her accusations, his threat
My crab-crawl for the stair
Their war cries through the locked door

Sunday morning Mass was different,
Quiet as an after-shock
Dulled by ritual Latin and an untuned choir
I settled down like sediment
While their anger began its old tick-tock.

Riverbank

'Almost the worst things have happened. . .'
    – Hubert Witheford, *Mosquitoes*

Sitting by the riverbank
Brown knees up to the sun
What a sweet well
    the sun drinks from

I recall what it was like
To dance naked in the streets

Her hair strokes the grass
The tide is out, the river
Rocks glisten and wink
    in a hot afternoon

When the city fell there
Was no warning, no escape

Her dress is gathered
Just below her waist
Recklessness of summer
    the warmed impulse

The gates collapsed, the sky
Darkened, I was running

Behind her shut lids
The river trickles to the sea
Lying on her arms
    in a dress of pink flowers

I imagined acts of bravery
Betrayal and fear are so ordinary.

Requiem

My father died quietly, without fuss
In a room drenched with apocalyptic light
We saw the last heaving of his chest
A sound like silk drawn through your fingers
As the bruised soul squeezed out between clenched
Teeth that had refused to part for days now
To whisper one word of the new world
He resisted through fevers and half-wakings
His hands scrawled mad hieroglyphs on the sheets
His claw-boned knees drew up the Mountains of the Moon
He became a continent no sane man would explore
And when the end came it was absurdly unremarkable
Without disturbing us, he simply went away
As if the ghost of him was all there had ever been
For so long invisible, a breath that came and went
Nothing more. His dying passed unnoticed
Until a lunatic whine pierced our lucky-bag
Memories of him. A sleek polished machine
Drew a line through his life, a set of green numbers
Gave the hour and the minute –
Latitude, longitude, we could pinpoint
The last place on earth he'd been seen alive
And this is what we talked about, what we remembered.

True North

Hearing for the first time that my grandfather's
Brother had drowned edging round Cape Horn

A sort of want starts up, as if the axis of the known
Had tilted. One more small thing needing a place

To fit. Boxing Day – above a snug wee graveyard
In a sloping field a man walks, rifle broken, with

His son. Time paces itself, a slow mist danders off.
The headstone names are local, a carved roll-call

Of certainties and what's what. I do not possess that,
A rooting gift, but clamber up to touch something like

It through the rigging of my doubt, feeling with every pitch
And squall the need to let go, fall free into what will

Absorb me, drown me. My True North is always shifting,
A few degrees from far off marks a considerable distance
   up close.

The Invaders

Shelter find and make it fit for winter
    light fires on high places and open hills
    we are here again, rough from loving
    the muscle cools, the marrow chills

New pens cut and write our histories
    twin gatherings of seeded doubt, frenzy
    we burned a season's length in briar beds
    jumped flame and water fearlessly

All caution strip away, unlock restraint
    the hopeless dead are risen at our beckoning
    for we are making merry on the tomb of love:
    the apple falls, the serpent slow unravelling

Evenings grow like appetites, we snigger
    at the earnest gape of lovers over tables
    we sharpened claw and fang on promises
    we know which phrases kill, which word disables

Blood us now among the laughing tribes
    the huddled back-seat courting innocents
    grass is greener, trees full-leafed because of us
    we are the choreographers of wishful circumstance.

Spiders

When these shelves were put up
when this wallpaper lay on the bed in rolls
we came here newly born each day to set it right
put our mark on each room and cast benevolent spells
in the hallway, hang a lamp over the door
one asked no more of the other
than to be the voice that answered in the dark

last night I startled spiders
with my tidying up, a modest family
bundled in a corner, so great their haste
to get away that the web vibrated, sang of them
for a time – I hear you telling me just where to drill
and what length the wood must be, how to measure up
a roll of paper so that I don't have to fight with it

no spells of forgetting keep you out
no amount of talking to myself brings you nearer
I brush away the web and feel I've achieved something.

Growing

Love was a worm gnawing at the apple
    buried in the heart of a hill

The bells of the cathedral hung like
    dark flowers, mute, still

Seasons became pages turned
    in a fading light, unread

Sea at his right hand, fields at his left
    snow at the foot of the bed

God in His kindness distributed the sun
    in freckles over the pale stones

Love was a maggot grown from
    the festering of dead love in the bone.

Stranger

When you speak Irish with her
I am put in my place
I am the stranger looking on

So much for all I know
A Planter's suspicion
Roots itself out from the gut

I sense secrets exchanged
Things said that I
Have no right to overhear

But I hear them
And cannot decipher them
Imagination is a sad scholar

So much for all I know –
This is what I am
An untongued foreigner.

Night Driving

I think of you through Omagh driving
the moon bewildered and all light gone out
up North where the maps of the heart change daily
that unsure territory of small towns and checkpoints
cold in that coat you said looked like a curtain
navigating the darkness, tuning the radio
hedges like ghosts flung out and hauled back
transmissions mauled by weather, distance, static

Rain ploughs the windscreen, the wipers metronomes
going home peels time from the gathered experiences
we are, for this is where the child has room
to manoeuvre in the phantom places maps won't mention:
but you are older now
and your feet can touch the floor
and behind each hedgerow soldiers, not trees,
stand to attention

The wind is a raw wound crying to be healed
drawing its long aching note over the Sperrins
into Derry, over church spires impaling low weather
few things are colder than the shut doors
of towns the harvests have abandoned
the rivers draw winter with them
like barges full of ice and solitude –
I wish you through all of this into the light and good

Cattle keep their heads down in the sodden fields
your twinned headbeams intersect the angles of a crossroads
here and there a road sign points into the earth
an articulated lorry hauls its mythic sea-mammal weight
over to the side and you slip past –
nearer now to familiar things,
gates that know your name and doors your keys can open
mirrors you've breathed on.

Anticipation

The water was warm enough for swimming
Toes in wet sand, bits of wrack and weed tickled
Not so bad here, but out a hundred yards or so
The colour changed and you could believe things
Hidden under that blue-green growl that would
Make you shudder: all around us a sky white
As a cheap soup-plate gleamed and sweated
No one and nothing moved in the afternoon
It was like being a child in a baker's shop
The heat, the anticipation, we waited with
A sort of arrogant content. Three of us, then,
Moving like comic figures, awkward, skinny
Into the sea, laughing, sand and salt avalanching
Off our spotty shoulders; strolled into the sea
Until it stopped us, pushed us back, and one
Of us fell still laughing at the daftness of it all
And disappeared where everyone could see
What was happening, but we never found him.

Song

Returning and parting,
Two sides of the same coin

The door to your house
Shut tight against love's intrusion

Grass yellows in the heat
Fire and love wither us

The two sides of us
Moon and sun, night and day

We are a half-lit room
A picture hanging at a slant.

Letter

for Saoirse

With pen and ink
    the tools to carve and course
    my small world
I furrow and loosen the clay of years
    and sink
In memory's dark
    the rusty iron of will and pride.

Weather gathers in my head
    convulsing the solid ground
    of hope and chance –
A dozen years, more, have cradled
    and fed
Dumb alienation
    a silence where the heart can hide.

Nearer

Onion-rings and cheese-burger in hot paper bags
coming up the canal, two o'clock in the morning
a clear night of fine-point stars, comfortably cold:
over the rooftops came *Nearer, My God, to Thee*

full-choired, an organ heaving under the voices
chimney smoke flimsy from fires going out
a weak ghost-light hanging in the empty streets
untrackable verses running up the dark like flags

I called you to the door: the music stopped.
A radio, you said, or someone playing records.
But the who or why is not important. I fidgeted
sleepless for hours while the room and the world

cradled gently from side to side.

Serious

I will not be the old gent in the fast-food café
At two in the morning.
Somehow or other I'll achieve something that will
Carry me beyond
The sound of cold plastic forks skewering and plastic
Knives raggedly cutting.
I will read a poem at four in the afternoon, listen
To Baroque music
Number among my closest friends lovers of art
And literature
And on Saturdays I'll take a girl to the cinema.

I will not wipe my sleeve across my chapped lips
And lurch for a taxi,
I will drive a car, leave my friends home first,
Have hot cocoa before bed.
Perhaps sleep will take longer as one gets older,
But one accepts that.
An encroaching, ambushing reluctance to face
Morning, that's all right.
I've noticed several good books on growing old
Alone, and if all else fails
There's a good all-night café close by – I'm not
Serious, of course.

Neighbours to the Renovated House
for Capt. C. Robert Hilton

A genial ghost turns the loft-ladder round
Small windows open and shut by themselves

Framed in the square panes a field of stones
Waist-high yellow grass waves in the garden

They tell you the next parish is Boston
This far West all light begins in water

They sing for you the families of this house
Names hard to weigh about an English tongue

There is the sound of hammering
Of sawing, of putting things back in place

The road slips a black line into the bay
A stray cow bellows at a broken gate

Sometimes there is nothing to fix, nothing
That isn't content and belonging of itself

You get to know the ebb and flow
The way the house has of saying yes or no

You begin to understand: scraps of their speech
Flutter like moths at the windows, soon

They will visit, bend under the low doorway
Stand in the renovated kitchen, take it all in.

Acquiring Culture

How we gather when we are called
Such hurried elegance sieved from a small town
We have come to honour the visiting poet
And we will not let him down

So much smaller and older he appears
In contrast, most definitely, with his audience
We will buy a copy of his book; for God's sake!
He might have shaved, it's common sense

But without him we would fall away
Into that small-farm, small-shop *gombeen* thing
That has us laughed at in our nation's capital –
We know our culture (the poet starts to sing!)

By God! The man's drunk! (How much was his fee?)
Next time for something like this have a vote
Set up a cultural committee: no one person alone
Should have the say, based merely on what a poet *wrote*

There are other considerations, our image
For instance – a poet should at least wear a tie
And some of his poems, well, a child could write them
Unless vetted first, a poet is not a very sound buy.

Two-Faced

They could stand up from the nets
throw an eye as far South as the blue mountains

and say This is mine, and that's his
and we've been here since God knows when.

My uncle would walk me to the harbour
his clipped throated speech would burrow

into my own. I would rehearse his *fash*
and *cran* and *th' day* in the car going home.

The Bible in my aunt's parlour was
as black and immoveable as Cave Hill

the names on its front pages crackled in
my mouth like potato-crisps. The wee house

looked over a clutch of fields towards the
lough, the townland names stubbornly Gaelic

No one mentioned history, it was like
a scarlet fever that had come and gone

it was in the past and mostly children got it.
It didn't plough fields, catch fish, or fix tractors

a planted pragmatism patchworked everything
you got the head down and the rest followed.

I had been born with a foot on either side
of the spade, I lived with an odd head-lightness

as if the slightest touch could unbalance me
toss me into the ditch. I could speak both languages

and consequently kept my mouth shut. I looked for
a sense of order and found random selection.

Even now, no one writes a word
about that lost tribe born two-faced, we have

no inheritance. I would watch my cousin's
tight-clamped knees, her white Sunday gloves

flowing over them like ice-cream. I envied
the redbricked schools, the cricket pitches

the plotted-out certainties, a way of walking
that I could manage on one leg only –

and so I went about in circles, a sort
of side-show to the main event, where everyone

else had his stage and knew his lines by heart
and knew his audience, no matter what.

I drew imaginary islands in my jotter,
peopled them, gave them language, history

modelled on what I was learning in school.
I pointed to the crayoned borders and said

out loud This is mine, and that's his
and gave them petty feuds to keep them busy.

My Da found me at it, the eye of John Wesley
shone out of his forehead, he grew afraid

that his son'd gone mad from adolescence.
Too much imagination's not good for you

he said. Two-minded, I threw the magic
books in the fire. Something savage came out

of the fields in protest. History recreated itself
one day at a time. Our hearth gods left us.

Two-cultured, I refused to define myself.
I was of the last generation to have choices.

Ships of Glass

My grandfather sailed in ships of glass
peered down and saw fields on the ocean floor

new-ploughed furrows and corn
chin up for the reaping currents; and odd fish

planting and cultivating, a whole season
under one right-left sweep of his officer's eye

he took to his room in his elder years
derided that plainfaced god of graceful ageing

blinding slowly from the light of medals
earned sending nourishment down to the sea acres

he'd once seen harvested, turned, sown –
he knew all comes to all, he began to swim

in tides of darkness that would lap his eyes
and make him gasp for air in his hourly sleeps

they came for him and yoked him to a plough
and made him walk a furrow or two for size

a hundred fathoms down he felt at home
better than that one-windowed back parlour

he'd been like a fish in a bowl, gape-mouthed
now he shook himself and breathed new air

walked tall in a kingdom he'd only imagined
took out his club secretary's pen and minuted

the aqueous mutterings of fish and the dead
waterwords melting and forming in his scaly head.

Good Weather
for Robert Welch

The harbour flat as a blackboard
our boat scribbled on it
we took advantage of good weather
went out in the afternoon to the lobster pots

our voices fell like bread on the water
the air tasted of honey
we curved our way among white
swans, fat as fullstops

we took off our shirts and vests,
let the sun run her tongue along our skin
you got odd Autumn days like this
unexpected, like an old love returned

other boats came up, we swapped
profanities, the land was so far back
we couldn't imagine it
arms idled elbow-deep over the sides

another day and everything could change
reduce each one of us
we'd watch the familiar rain and fret
drying up in windows like old flowers

so we learn to walk on water
our names written in salt
we dissolve in the liquid afternoon
get drunk on ourselves and sometimes sing.

Servants' Quarters

Their routine is still
visible, laid out
on the busy air
like drying blankets

you are made aware
of perfect duty
angels on a ladder
climbing the stone stair

peacocks strut
the length of a shed roof
proof, if any were needed
of nature's pecking order

gardens unweeded
the yard-bell rusted tight –
they threw open other
people's windows

nursed bodies
they would never own
blinked
in someone else's light.

Transfiguration

'The sea is no place to be if you can help it. . .'
    – W.H. Auden, *The Enchafèd Flood*

I am the sea, she said: come swim in me.
Remember Auden's dreamy dissertation

I am change and upheaval, things disturbed
the living opposite of stability.

I am moon, tides, the shell forming
from sheer imagination – I despise the rock

that sits in its solidness like a proposition
of mathematics – I am something

very different. She stretched out her arms
and pirouetted on the soft, wet sand,

with that laugh again I'd known in music
when each instrument informs

the other of the miracle of harmony
and tone. We are too quick

to despise moonlight, she said, it finds
us out, it is fire turned by alchemy

into silver. Look how it paints
my fingernails, and I have lived in caves

of pure fire, I am dangerous and immune
to common order and civil restraints –

a sea breeze woke us, sand in our hair
her arms were over me and she murmured

that love was chaos, turbulence,
night was its natural thoroughfare –

letters of lunacy burned on our skin
our parched tongues lapped salt

we wiped sand from our eyes and heard
the breathy lullaby of boats coming in.

Light out of Smoak
for Seán Ó Murchú

Horace commented that Homer could 'fetch light out of Smoak',
according to Robert Wolseley (1685)

In the dark wood, a fox has a child's face
no miracle, just what you'd expect

that predictable conjuring of survival
we do similar things to bewitch our pursuers

there is a language of camouflage
a leafy net pulled over true meaning

too dark, I suspect, the literal wood
hob-goblin absolutes too numerous, scary

no great wonder, then, this New Age
search, Oriental back-rubs, *The Celtic Tarot*

palm-readings, ubiquitous
printed cards advertising inner child healing

we change ourselves, or try to, and find
the bogeymen changing with us – they too

appreciate disguises.
We could conjure light out of smoke,

shed our skins, go back to a first utterance
when nothing need be understood

here, wordless, we say, we were happy
the world's teat quenched our thirst

who gave us language caused the trouble
we named ourselves, bit deep into the apple

we swallowed the worm at the core,
absorbed the squirm and slither of fear

to go back, then, to spit it out
would be salvation of a worthwhile sort.

But no. The shadow lies on the threshold.
We call for new magic to dilute the darkness

it grows thicker, begins to speak:
All these years a fox in the trees,

a changeling, yet the dogs are never far off.
Learn their names, they'll eat from your hand.

But the woods are warmer, we can breathe
more easily here. We need no words at all now

with our noses in the wet earth. No language.
This bark will do. Abrupt, loud, it says it all.

Black

Black, she said, the nights I must endure
in shadow cast the corners of the room
vast distances of cold lightlessness
crossed once and never forgotten
the shapeless curtained silence of a tomb

Then, when he comes, black his thoughts
he strips the bedroom of its sanctity
nails go through my feet into the walls
I am spreadeagled, a skinned thing
a trophy, triumph of his animosity –

Outside black wings beat and birds
like sins coagulate on the surface of the sky
I remember childhood and my porridge-
definition of the soul: night-bells sound
the world extinguished like a candle or a cry.

Music

for Máirtín O Connor

We talk about it in some fashion
every time we meet
the characteristics of the Irish psyche
low-hung weather like muslin over the eyes
a tendency to think too much about ourselves
and what this sun-lack does to poetry

a grainy drift of history
moves over the pier at Annaghdown
Raftery's sung dead under the blowy water
the note wind makes on the lip of a reed
the shape of music working in the bone –
the sacrament of dreaming turned to sound.

She Has No Need Of The Rose

She has no need of the rose, her spell
derives from things too personal to tell –

She talks over coffee of a torrid divorce
her husband was, by all accounts, coarse

And given to violent, unprovoked rage
All in all, he was close to twice her age

Her attraction grows with each detail
One's powers of moral discernment fail

A monster, of course, to treat her that way –
I snatch up the bill and call a waiter to pay

We stand, and her triumph rings out like a bell
She pins our table's pitiful rose in my lapel.

Grassroots

'A world brought back to scale, a house to order.'
    – Micheal O Siadhail, *A Circle*

In a window over the front door
an arms-out Child of Prague saw us off
Saturday night under Clery's clock
refugees like us rushed forward at every bus

we went to Mass together, had tea
played a sort of messy acrobatics on the sofa
listening for a key scraping a lock
a taxi door slamming, a gate whining maliciously

the world had a set geometry, rules
gave shape to possible chaos, love tailored
like a sports-jacket, no difference
between *tight* and *snug* –

I lied to get away, had to, really
did the best thing in the circumstances
I'd come with my hand out for certainties
and thrashed now at their rootedness

no more Sundays round that table
a future planned in accordance with a law
already rotting on the page, no more
cutting my hair to a respectable length

I wore US Army shirts and grew a beard
I knew the drift was on, felt it start
to pull me from that once-cherished place
to some other, darker harbour of the heart.

Columbus in Galway
for Tim Dennehy

Sweet Bianchinetta, a year has passed
since I saw two ships consumed by fire
and heard the drowning and the burning sounds
and lay half dead in Portugal –

here, I can think of it and not shake,
I do not lie awake much and the weather's kind
I find myself listening to the sea again
not hearing now those other noises underneath

the talk in the streets is all of trade
with Compostela brokers wine-eyed, everywhere;
the slightest off-shore storm and a ship's delayed
money's lost and merchants haggle in their doors

there are cartographers here who say a map
has been developed that can chart the Ocean Sea
from what has been dreamed over and imagined
of worlds so steeped in nature no god is necessary

and for myself, sweet sister, I've half a mind
to take them on and peruse their parchment scrawls
distil the rumours and the back-street bragging
outfit a vessel and see what they dream about –

but not just now – I'll take my time
and let the Indies murmur in their sleep:
someone's cried the watch and rung the hour
and soft rain presses like a finger on the glass.

Faith

I will meet a girl with shining hair –
so says my horoscope in *The Star*

after Mass, a woman whispers of
miracles in Bosnia, the blind will see

we hedge our bets: God as *croupier*
there are new demons at the tables

we can talk with equal innocence
about the Bundesbank and fairies

this child's soul-carelessness
makes murder and magic easy

I am always two people: I bless
myself outside a church, I do not

allow whitethorn in the house –
I fear what cannot be proved

and shrug off that which is –
there is a stone in me that cannot be removed.

Language Classes
on hearing of the death of George MacBeth

Notebooks and coffee, a dry anticipation.
It's been twenty-three years since I felt all this
or understood the need for discipline
outside the poetic or the spoken word –

this small learning will travel with us,
tame more passionate tongues in sunnier places
try the old used bluff of pretending
that language is symmetrical and can be measured

your death, meanwhile, had filtered down
a 'phone-line from the BBC, someone listening
for something else heard the report on the news,
you'd spent good years there, so you told me

the time we sank in those monstrous lobby chairs
my note-taking hurried, catching up,
netting in all those dates and names, playing
at journalist again, needing shoes

that sense of style, you said, a poet
should cultivate for himself, not like
the rest, he is something specific –
it was something you carried over from another

time, offering all of it, knowing
the deserving and the dull are indistinguishable
in the soft light of something new, and it takes
too much time and effort to sort them out

break them down to constituent parts –
all morning I've been learning to speak English
again, to pass ragged syntax and eccentric verbs
on down the line to a world unaware of the *TLS*

to mate subject, verb, object, in some half-
decent comprehensible form; hearing over it all
the metronome of your walking-cane
marking time to an older music.

Pizza

Dark flecked with snow –
the Midland villages, one street and a video store
I see a movie hero leer from a window
cardboard, but a human face: nothing more

I am in Ireland
its night-filled, clock-ticking, unrepentant heart
history's naked bulb swings back and forth
over the face of an unDublinised people

It is a place to have
nothing to say, a speechlessness from birth
the click-clack of balls on a snooker table
in a pub where the big buses stop

I hear poets on the radio
discussing football, current affairs, the world
as if nothing lived west of Leixlip
Ireland as a Sunday outing, that other place

Maria, heart, you spoke of buses
taking that long run down from the Hill
of the Foreigner – I feel the curtain of your
country close behind me

Those lost hours
slack-eyed over the lurch and tug –
your Ireland puts on make-up and meets
this little pizza-slice of Europe with a smile.

Green

'Love for the virtue, which attended me
E'en to the palm, and issuing from the field. . . .'
   – Dante, *Paradise (The Divine Comedy) Canto XXV*

I sat upstairs with my dufflebag on my lap
my lust, like some small irritated animal, concealed
it was the last of my summers, the hills bright green
a stretch of toffee-coloured road hung out like washing
Latin conjugations tumbled in the basin of memory
I would invent a new language for you, juggle history

                    I wrote your name out three times,
whispered the word to conjure you into my room, between
the Airfix fighters dangling on threads from the ceiling
and the all-reflecting mirror

What difference did it make to the anonymous world
revamping our two histories nightly on the black-and-white TV
that I saw an angel preen his courtly feathers under
a concrete streetlamp, spit-polish his sword
as your green bus from Lisnasharragh coughed up the hill?
No summer held its breath like that again, or will.

Waste Ground

Over the waste ground you hear them snigger
    midnight priests of public house and bookmaker
    what we are reduced to, this atavistic laughter

Let us worship the broken window and its memory
    the shattered door, the tabernacle cracked, empty
    the teenage lovers hand-in-glove with new misery

Let us define all things according to their names
    mad dogs are nosing in our waste-disposal bins
    a voice yells out of nowhere: *Bring out the guns*

Bring out the dead who haunt the broken armchair
    release the hideous neon birds of the video air
    to peck our children's eyes to a blind man's stare

Let us build shrines to our beer-bellied martyrs
    who hard-men their way as husbands and fathers
    over the waste ground hang their football banners

For nothing lives here that has its own country
    no passport but a dole card is required to move freely
    I am of Ireland: but all that means here is history

Hang out the lamps that mark where traps are laid
    under a moon razored like a bottle broken on a head
    mop up its overspill of morbid pity: do not be afraid.

Indifference

Forced indifference makes fools of us both.
The right thing is seldom said (nor should it be)
What is love but strangeness brought to bed
And offered gifts, to set another strangeness free?

And you for whom no love is love enough
May speculate on whether this or that man pleases
By look, by dress, by turn of conversation judged
When warmed beneath such heartlessness, he freezes.

Yet I am lover also, in my silent fashion
Who offers nothing, but is better off besides
I'm used by now to clinging to love's rock
And waiting for the rescue of your fickle tides.

Roofbeams

'*Cut in these Trees their Mistress name. . .*'
   – Andrew Marvell, *The Garden*

Under the peeled skin this worn bone
  pushed through, moved out towards a light
forgotten
       taking for an hour or so that day
a thin caress of rain, being itself in a way
impossible under the nailed weight of covering

How long in the dark, to approach
  a natural blindness? The seams and whorls
retract, condense
       the odour of smoke splinters upwards
dissolves in a watery February afternoon –
we pull away our ladders under a fall of stars

And I walk home by the road I know best
  chilled in the dark, remembering somehow
for no sound reason
       the noise a beam made when a hammer
punished it, a cry, perhaps an appeal
which, unreadable, sounded even louder

And feel unsure of myself out of my years
  as if, opening our door, I'll know the silence
for what it hides
       so much layered under the obvious
I'd misinterpreted what shape the surface took
for what held it all together: you, me, the frame of us.

Dark

White swans like tacks on a board
Bridges idle, odour of drains
Love and death danced here
       Nothing remains

Sleep with the window half-open
Something vague moves on a ledge
A paperback on the floor
       A marked page

A girl's laugh perforates all this
Tedious motion of dark into light
Imagine her in the act of love
       Nothing polite

Black birds settle in the quiet trees
The last door closes with a slam
A moon intrudes like a comma –
       I am, I am.

Lines Inspired By A Drinking Song

Sarah by the window, the sun slanting
drawing slow evening with it, a summer day
going down at the end of the garden
and the smell of grass and earth and hedge

Sarah, my joy night and morning

canvas drawn tight on a frame, painting
until all light goes out, a kettle jigging under
the half-open window; I arrive, intruder,
as she cools the hot tea with her breath

Sarah, my joy night and morning

that small house of small warm rooms
her legs tucked under, she sits and listens
painted fingers curled about the cup, my words
flail the dry kitchen air, I fidget, so full of her

Sarah, my joy night and morning

older, I lie and wait for the sun, watery, dim,
an old man's eye blind to a new world
my books, my tannin-stained mug, my ink
flooding everything with half-tones of reproach

Sarah, my joy night and morning

I hear rumours of Sarah like news from a war
sieved through the mouths of strangers, cold,
colourless, as if those furious glows and tints
had been bled from her and she were shadow.
Sarah, my joy night and morning.

Ashes

From here a wave travels for miles
Over a plain of small farms, figures
Round the outbuildings, fields painted
In a light green wash, blue roads
Wrapping it all in tidy bales

As if nothing matters, I lose myself
In a dream of belonging, my hands
Oiled from tractor work, high boots
Muddied I move to a corrugated shed
Feel this work's rhythm, a slow pulse

I'd stand at the gate and stroke the dark
Know each neighbour by his cap
Slowly feel the tug of age and silence –
No recompense in being close to nature
My heart annointed with her ashes-mark.

Horizonal

'Oh, said I, my friend and lover
take we now that ship and sail. . . .'
    – Housman, *The Land of Biscay*

If I watch the sea's horizon long enough
How long, love,

before the boat I see is yours?

How long before her moon-mad crew
Raise their shout of coming home

and put up their oaken oars?

And how long before our little house of salt
Can breathe again

through open windows, open doors?

In the Workshop

for Paul Wilkins

It begins here. Air trapped in resin
Curled blonde wood on a pocked bench
A gape-jawed clamp catching an oily light

The sound of assuming form and shape
Dry rustle of tidy packets of gauged strings
Hanging on a plastered wall, new fiddles

And repaired guitars: old tunes are
Removed and polished, new ones find
The right depth and grip. Everything waits.

Docklands

'Fios a d'fhionnais ó chlann an duig. . . . .'
  – Máirtín Ó Direáin, *An Stailc*

Docklands were tribal, assured
aloof gantries, cranes under orders
hierarchy of hoist, pulley, steel cable

It closes down, grass in the rails
a shutter flapping out a single chord, a white
bird tossing like a rag in the blue air

And men – I know some of them – bend
against the salted wind, smoke, screw up their
faces, make loser horse-race jokes

Their backs turned to what's sinking
all-hands; no word for all that's gone under,
no need to lock gates on the lost forever.

Flood

*'There was a picture of Yeats' tower in the paper
this morning, surrounded by water.'*
   – Letter

No doves came back
The houses rode like arks
For days

Local politicians like hooded birds
Sat up in rowing boats and made themselves visible

The floodlands spread
Silver under a lead sky
Acres dissolved

Their televised despair stayed with you
Men whose faces puckered under rain and fear

The West of Synge,
Yeats, the house at Coole
Slobbered up by a bad winter

No slain chieftains to rise murderously and restore
The demolished pastures, no comforting mythologies

Here we lie at the mercy
Of weather, of crass mortality
Unlike anything you've ever read.

Paraphrase

Something we do or refuse to do locks the night away
Your pale goodbyeing hand against the green paint of
The door, the rhyming swing of windscreen wipers
Hymning their Gothic paraphrase: *No more, no more*

And so to bed, as if the very act of pillowing my head
Were sufficient to cure all agues of soul and heart
While outside over the rooftops an acned moon stops
Turning the tossed coin of itself: *Decide, decide*

When clocks alarm and banter their way about
A new day of sorts promises itself, with no guarantees
Socks unchanged and underwear so-so, we heave and go
Sturdy mariners adrift in quotidian undertow: *Name names*

So I name you to myself as I start and choke the car
Highwayman ready and waiting for the road to rise
A flighty wingy flap of pigeons scared up from under
The wheels announces my lift-off: *Gently, gently.*

Gift

A gift for working at the circle's edge
Has her striding like a girl through broken fields
    Long before the likes of us are up
    Whose feet are planted in a sadder clay
    Sunk under the weather, we refuse the day

Driving heavy cattle out of our ridged garden
Voicing off abrupt and loud like a dealer in a row
    Making easy what the unused heart
    Turns shyly from, we hearing but unable
    To do more than set a late breakfast table

Not allowing for the shock of things
That have their feeling from such earthed routine
    We sugar tea with unbecoming quiet
    Avoid the clack and banter of spoon and cup –
    She closes back the gate, lets the iron latch drop.

Barn

We walk by the stone barn
Here an iron wheel rim, here
Barrel hoops, a scythe chipped in rust
Wood dust scurries roofward at the opening
door
    a set of woven creels, a ladder shaking
    as he works up a dozen rungs, then
    hesitates at the planked loft floor

We leave it in its quiet waking
A red roof beaconing over a stone bog
A flight of steps outside and rocked-up windows
Call out an urge to inhabit, make alive, bring
light
    through every arched and lifted corner
    resettle the solid stillness, break the lock
    that manacles the held air, put things right.

Derrykyle, Spring 1996

Parting in Winter

'*Drowsing in my chair of disbelief. . . .*'
    – Robert Graves, *The Visitation*

Parting in Winter is no treason –
Leaf from branch,
Snow from window ledge,
You from me –
It is the name of the season

I sit at a table near a window
Wait while
Meat is cut from bone
Steam rises
Fork-work leaves a neat furrow

On moist vegetables: snow
Is promised,
We eat and drowse –
I feel closer
To what I will not, can not, know.